STARS
IN
JARS

For Warren, Esther, Sam and Liz

First published 2014 by A & C Black,
an imprint of Bloomsbury Publishing Plc
50 Bedford Square
London WC1B 3DP

www.bloomsbury.com

This collection copyright © 2014 A & C Black
Text copyright © 2014 Chrissie Gittins
Illustrations copyright © 2014 Calef Brown

The right of Chrissie Gittins and Calef Brown to be identified as the author and illustrator of this work has been asserted by them in accordance with the Copyrights, Designs and Patents Act 1988.

ISBN 978-1-4081-9693-9

A CIP catalogue for this book is available from the British Library.

Printed and Bound by CPI Group (UK) Ltd, Croydon CR0 4YY

1 3 5 7 9 10 8 6 4 2

Chrissie Gittins

STARS IN JARS

New and Collected Poems

Illustrated by Calef Brown

A & C BLACK
AN IMPRINT OF BLOOMSBURY
LONDON NEW DELHI NEW YORK SYDNEY

Contents

Sky-High

For Vincent

William went up in a rocket
to see where it would go.
It flew round
             and round
                       and round
the sun,
and burnt his left big toe.

Then he flew around the moon,
to see if it was made of cheese.
It crash-landed
             in some camembert,
and William hurt his knees.

Then he flew through the Milky Way
and caught
             a trail of stars.
He brought them home
to
his
cosy
house,
where he keeps them safe in jars.

High-Chair

for Alice Catherine

Arms up
Bib on
Eat up
Get down

Arms up
Bib on
Throw food
Mum down

Arms out
No bib
Get down
Throw up

Dad tries
No go
Head down
Give up

Sam, Sam, Quite Contrary

Sam, Sam, quite contrary,
bought a budgie,
wanted a canary.

Sam, Sam, quite contrary,
kissed Suzannah,
meant to kiss Mary.

Sam, Sam, quite contrary,
dressed as a pirate,
playing a fairy.

Sam, Sam, quite contrary,
ate dark chocolate,
says he likes dairy.

Sam, Sam, quite contrary,
shaved his head,
to make it hairy.

The Tale of Dotty Cuddletum

There was a young girl called Lottie
whose tum was ever so spotty,
she pulled up her vest
inspected her chest
and then went to sit on her potty.

The spots were all over her arms and her legs,
she even had one on her nose.
When she took off her socks
and wiggled her feet
she had seventeen spots on her toes.

"Don't worry," said Mummy,
"Don't worry," said Daddy,
"we'll go to the shop tomorrow
for a bottle of potion called calamine lotion
then we'll just see how it goes."

By the end of the week,
the treatment complete,
Lottie was not quite so spotty.
She patted her tum and began to have fun
from that day her nickname was Dotty.

Twister Hamster

Twister sleeps in the day,
Esther sleeps at night.
Esther wakes in the morning,
gives Twister quite a fright
by poking her finger at Twister
who bites her thumb real hard.

Esther now has a plaster.
And she pulls away her finger a bit faster.

Harry the Hamster

Harry the hamster, in his ball,
rolled round the bedroom,
rolled round the hall.
He rolled to the bathroom,
he rolled to the stairs
where a huge teddy bear
took him clean unawares.

He rolled slap-bang into
the honey hall wall,
but that didn't stop him
for he was so small
and a whole world awaited
Harry in his ball.

On Monday he rolled down the garden,
on Tuesday he rolled down the road,
on Thursday he rolled down a bike path
till he was stopped in his tracks
by a toad.

On Friday he rolled to New Brighton,
on Saturday to warm Singapore,
on Sunday he yawned, climbed back
in his cage, and all day
simply rolled in his straw.

Suzannah the Tail Wagger

soar.
spirits
their
make
to
way
fire
sure
a
is
wag
tail
a
blue,
feeling
is
them
of
one
If
labrador.
beloved
her
of
tail
the
wags
wagger
tail
the
Suzannah

The Well-Travelled Tortoise

I am a tortoise from Turkey,
I lived in the hills of Kalkan,
my name over there was Mustafa,
my owners here call me Ken.

I would squaffle in the leaves on the slopes,
taking days from A to B,
the sun beat down on my back,
my nostrils were full of the sea.

Here in Catford it's different,
I live in a circular pen,
I walk the ten-metre circumference
and then walk round it again.

Instead of the calling to prayers
I hear the South Circular cars,
the sky is filled with neon,
there are hardly any stars.

I miss the smell of pine,
bougainvillaea dripping purple and red,
but here I get lots of attention,
I admit it has gone to my head.

A Goldfish Remembers

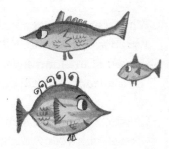

Being carried from the fair
in a see-through plastic bag,
being plopped into a bowl
with another golden lad.

Swimming round a pot pagoda
and a quivering piece of weed,
watching my owner watch the telly –
he thinks he's the referee!

Watching my owner watching me
each and every hour,
waking up to cloudy water –
it tasted very sour.

Waking up without my mate
because he jumped out of the bowl,
wondering where on earth he's gone,
and where's his goldfish soul?

Seeing him on the carpet,
frozen stiff and still.
Thinking that won't happen to me –
I'm going to live until

I'm 43!
My name is Tish,
I'm from the North.
You just wait and see!

A goldfish remembers memories for 3 months. Tish, from North Yorkshire, was the Guinness Book of Records' longest-living goldfish.

When I Was Tiny

When I was a tiny baby,
even before I was born,
I swam in my mummy's tummy,
I swam from dusk till dawn.

I swam with purple armbands,
I swam with yellow ducks,
I swam with a clockwork turtle
and orange dumper trucks.

Now I swim in a swimming pool,
I splish and splosh and splash,
I kick my legs and spread my arms –
I never need a wash!

When I climb in the bath tub,
I have a wooden boat with sails,
the water gets real choppy –
what with crocodiles and whales.

But my favourite place for swimming
is the frothy fizzy sea.
I like to chase the gentle waves,
and then the waves chase me!

I Want to be My Baby Brother

I want to waddle without a nappy,
neatly miss my potty.
I want smears of Marmite round my mouth.

I want you to blow raspberries on my belly,
suck my fingers, throw me in the air.
I want a currant biscuit in each hand,

another crunched in the carpet,
crispy crumbs between my toes.
I want to sit in the bath with a tipper,

I want to pull the leaves off lilies,
I want to lie on your back
with my head in the dip of your neck.

I want to scream so loud when I can't catch
the butterfly that your ears hurt.

My Older Brother

My brother jumps on me,
pushes me,
pulls me,
hits me,
shouts at me,
rolls me over.

He kisses me,
cuddles me,
reads me stories,
makes me laugh – ha ha ha.
Makes me cry.

Then buys me a bracelet from his school trip to Wales.

My Cousin

My cousin is a robot,
she has metal in her knee,
she gets rusty in the morning
before her cup of tea.

She grows a wealth of flowers
in earth that's rich and deep,
and when her flowers flourish
my cousin takes a leap

across the wide Long Mynd,
which rises by Church Stretton.
She leans against the wind,
until her elbows flatten.

I Don't Want an Avocado for an Uncle

I don't want an icicle for an auntie,
she might snap.

I don't want a tomato for an older brother,
he might go red in the face.

I don't want a candle for a gran,
she might melt.

I don't want a coffee bean for a cousin,
he might get swallowed from a cup.

I don't want a blister for a sister,
she might get sore.

I don't want an avocado for an uncle,
he might go squishy.

I don't want a carpet for a granddad,
he might be threadbare.

I don't want a plum for a mum,
she might get made into chutney.

I don't want a diamond for a dad
because he'd be the hardest man in the world.

My Grandma is a Nun

My grandma picks the blackberries,
the plums and apples too,
she feeds the ducks
and feeds the hens,
she sees the morning dew
before she goes to say the prayers
for me, and you, and you.

She writes on her computer,
she reads great big thick books,
she makes the jam and chutney
and helps out other cooks.

At weekend she plans the menu,
picks parsley, chives and thyme,
my grandma is a fun nun,
and apart from God's, she's mine.

Fidget Pie

If you fuss and fiddle,
I'll bake you in a pie.

If you fume and flap,
You'll soon be wondering why

I baked you in a pie.

Throw a fit of fury,
A flurry or a fret,
I'll cover you in pastry,
Squirt a jet of gravy,

So when you froth and foam,
In a fiery frenzied moan,
You'll still be wondering why,

I baked you in a pie!

Fidget pie – originally a pie made in Shropshire; it used to be called a 'fitched' pie because that meant it had five sides or five corners.

Gutted

These flats. I'm getting out of here.
I'm not going to be one of those they come round
collecting for wreaths for.

I want a room of my own.
Sean even gets hold of my underpants
if I don't watch him. And I'm sick of his City posters.

Telly's rubbish in the day. The adverts are alright.
I want to spear a dummy with a bayonet.
I bet my dad was in the army,
I bet he had boots and a gun.
I would stand to attention, I would
salute with my hand like this.

I wish I wasn't the eldest.
Sometimes I go to the fridge and drink
the baby's milk from her bottle.

My Dad's More Embarrassing Than Your Dad

My dad's more embarrassing than your dad.
Does yours get all your friends' names wrong?

My dad has to be more embarrassing than your dad.
Does yours try to sing your favourite song?

My dad is way more embarrassing than your dad.
Does yours wear sandals with socks on the sands?

My dad is so more embarrassing than your dad.
Does yours dance with just his feet and his hands?

My dad is definitely more embarrassing than your dad.
Does yours always ask how to use the computer?

My dad is a trillion times more embarrassing than your dad.
Does yours try to wiggle his hooter?

I Can't Fix Everything

I can fix the picnic basket,
the sticky window in your room,
I can fix your seventh puncture,
I can fix that very soon,

but I can't fix the weather
when we're sitting on the sand
and the rain beats down
leaving holes behind.

I can fix the squeaky door
and the stain on your rug,
I can fix your seagull mobile
and the handle on your mug,

but I can't fix the fall out
with the friend you've had for years,
I can only nurse the hurt
and wipe away the tears.

I can fix a fallen shelf
and a wonky wooden bed,
I can fix a crashed computer
and that wall you painted red,

but I can't fix it when you fall in love
with someone who doesn't feel the same.
I can only say, 'Pick another',
fall in love again.

The Best Hiding Place in the World

I'm crouching in my hiding place,
my mum is going wild,
she's traipsing up and down the aisles,
"Where are you, naughty child?"

I'm counting up the soap powders –
the liquid and the blocks,
they line the shelves opposite,
they clean my jeans and socks.

Mum's voice is getting louder,
the manager gets called,
he sends a message to the store,
(he's tall and very bald).

"If you see a little girl,
dressed in a purple top,
please inform the manager,
then our search can stop."

Game's up, I'm caught –
been seen through the holes,
I'm hiding on the bottom shelf –
behind the toilet rolls!

The Way He Used To Be

I miss the way my brother used to be,
he'd flop back on the sofa,
somersault on the lawn,

he punched the air,
gave me a high five
when he won the football game.

All of a sudden
he'd clear the living room,
push back the table,

put on rock music
and wiggle his bottom from side to side.
I laughed till I cried.

He painted wicked pictures
with robots and kangaroos,
he held my hand

when we crossed the road,
he never let me lose
at snap or dominoes.

I miss the way my brother used to be,
the way he stuck out his tongue,
the way he cuddled me.

Necklace

I had a row with my mum,
stormed off up the stairs,
I really was sorry
to make her worry,
staying out late
without a word.

I tidied my room
and cleaned the shoes,
and made my own packed lunch.
I picked her flowers
and swept the floor
and then I had a hunch.

I could mend her broken necklace,
the one her grandma gave.
I threaded the beads one by one
and counted off the days.

The day we rode on donkeys,
rattling down the beach,
the day she made me chocolate cake
and hid it out of reach,

the day she smoothed my forehead,
when a fever raged inside,
the day I held an egg and spoon
and she cheered me on with pride.

I gave my mum the necklace,
she wrapped her arms around.
In that delectable moment,
you could not hear a sound.

The Handkerchief Tree

This one's for the sniffles,
when your nose runs down to your mouth,
this one's for the blues,
when the sides of your mouth run south.

This one's for strawberry cheesecake icecream,
it's so good you just have to dribble,
this one's for your left-over-sandwich –
there was only time for a nibble.

This one goes round your knee
when you've fallen off your bike,
this one's for when you slip on the pitch –
but it was worth it for that strike.

This one's to give your mum
when you start your first day at school,
and this one's for when you fall in love
and you feel an absolute fool.

To My Daughter, As She Learns to Play the Qin

(from 'Feeling from Mountain and Water', an animated Chinese film by Te Wei)

I will teach you as I was taught.

An old man came down the mountain,
leaning in the wind.
I caught him when he stumbled.

His music met mine, he laid his qin before me.
Orange leaves feathered the air,
by snowfall I could play.

When the frog swelled his chest and
fishes gathered at a worm
we left to sail the slanting gorge.

Monkeys jumped in trees,
stones split falling water.
I didn't want to say goodbye.

I clutched him close,
then knelt and took the qin
bequeathed to me.

He left as he had come.
From up on high I plucked the strings,
filled the valley with his gift.

I will teach you well, as I was taught.

Qin (pronounced 'chin'): a plucked seven-string Chinese musical instrument of the zither family.

Pencil Stub

for William Patten School

When I was new I drew
the leather shoe lace on a magic shoe.

You shaved me down.

I wound my lead around
the leaves of an ancient
willow tree.

You shaved me down.

I drew a circle, you
rubbed me out,
It became a careful square.

You shaved me down.

I was happiest tracing
the face of your mother –
her plaited hair,
her sparkling slate grey eyes.

And still you shaved me down.

I could conjure the universe,
skirt Saturn with a silver ring,
chase the rain falling from
a shooting star.

A Memory of Snow

for Esther

That night the gale tilted the foreshore,
    wide rain spat at the hills,
        you turned in your thin deep bed,
            asleep with staring eyes.

        As snow rose up the mountains,
      scree on peaks washed through,
    you dreamt of herons on goatherds,
of the way a buzzard flew.

You woke to six bare mountains,
    to one with a memory of snow,
        to sheep climbing the staircase,
            to blink at a face they know.

        A stag came into the garden,
      he bowed his head to the ground,
    dislodged his rack of antlers –
his gift for you to find.

Possible Presents

The lick of a tall ice cream
and the first burnt nose of summer.

The jumper which shrunk in the wash
back to its usual size.

A bowl of red tulips
which curl up their petals at night.

A camouflaged frog jumping
between caramel leaves.

Bread baked this morning
spread with Somerset butter.

The blackbird which sings in the tree
each day at a quarter to four.

My Friend Bob

For Barlby Primary School, North Kensington

My friend Bob
is always there,
he doesn't turn
a single hair
if I'm lonely or sad,
or if I wake like a bear
with a very sore head.

My friend Bob
is loyal and true,
wherever I go –
to the park, or the zoo,
he comes too –
we see penguins waddle
and the lions being fed.

He tells me how
to play the game,
when to dribble,
when to shoot,
when to pass the ball.
If I score he cheers
loudest of all,
till my poor round face
goes tomato red.

My friends all know about
my friend Bob,
they ask how he is,
and who is his Dad?
He doesn't have a home,
he lives with me.
He has a very comfy place
inside my head!

Getting Up

Time to get up, Sam.

The sun shines through my red curtains
like an electric fire,
Noddy cocks his head beside my bed – tick tock.
I snuggle up to Mr Snowman.
He walks across my duvet, nice and warm.

Come on, Sam, time to get up.

Where did I put my t-shirt?
It was on the bookshelf,
maybe it ran for cover under the bed.
Oh look, there's my teddy, John.
What's it like living under there?

Sam, get yourself dressed,
you're going to be late for school.

Expect you'd like some breakfast,
would bread and honey do the trick?
Or mashed banana in a sandwich, yum.
I need to tie your bow around your neck.

Sam, if you're not down here in two
minutes, you're in big trouble.

Where's the armhole in this jumper?
I know I had another sock,
maybe Toucan knows who hid my trouser.
I know, I'll wear my Batman outfit,
without socks.

You can't go to school like that, Sam.

Why not? Why not? Why not?

Going to be Late for School

It's hard to walk fast in the morning
when there's a washing machine in my tummy.

It churns and swirls my toast and jam,
while I jump the cracks in the pavement.

Three more turnings to go –
my tea is rinsing my Frosties.

Mums and dads walk towards me,
the lollipop lady has gone.

I launch into a flat spin,
hang up my coat,

race to my classroom –
the register has just begun.

Gillian Costigan

I wish I was Gillian Costigan,
with hair brushed sleek
and clothes that fit.
I wish I was Gillian Costigan
with money in my pocket every single week.

Her smile is wide,
her shoes have a shine,
she has friends to tea,
she laughs all the time.

I wish I was Gillian Costigan.
She has holidays in Greece,
her dad loves her mum,
she has nieces and nephews,
a nan and a gran,
her sarnies are thick
with hard cheese and ham.

I wish I was Gillian Costigan
with a slide in my hair,
a huge mum to hug me,
a new top to wear.

Three

My best friend has a best friend,
she is a bester friend than me,
but when they have a falling out
my friend is best with me.

Dawn Meets the Queen

The chandeliers were like upside-down sparkly trees,
the sofas were as long as stretch limousines.

I sunk, waist-deep, in red carpet,
nibbled miniature scones.

Watched by her Rembrandt and Vermeer
the Queen came near. She smiled.

"And which school are you from?
Are you enjoying your visit?"

I ran to my teacher.
"I've just spoken to THE QUEEN!"

My mouth was as wide as Japan.
"Really, she's just like my nan!"

Queens

for Tess

One day, while out walking,
the Queen of Asking Stupid Questions met
the Queen of Stating The Obvious.
"Are you walking to town?" asked the Queen of Asking.
"This is such a long road," said the Queen of Stating,
peering at the spires in the distance.
The sky was purple and grey.

"Will it rain, do you think?" asked the Queen of Asking.
"This umbrella is full of holes," said the Queen of Stating.
Her curls dripped down her cheeks.

"Will it take long?" asked Asking.
"As long as it takes," said Stating.

When Is a Boy Not a Boy?

for Oswald and Selhurst Boys

When is a boy not a boy?
When he's a plank of wood.

When is a boy a plank of wood?
When he goes rigid with fear.

When does a boy go rigid with fear?
When he's being carried across the river.

When is a boy carried across the river?
When he's the smallest in a party of boys being chased by
bullocks.

When is a boy part of a party of boys being chased by bullocks?
When they're being taken for a walk to the nearest village
by their history teacher.

*When is a boy taken for a walk to the nearest village by his
history teacher?*
When he's staying in a thatched farmhouse to do creative
writing in the middle of Devon.

*When does a boy stay in a thatched farmhouse to do creative
writing in the middle of Devon?*
When he's capable of becoming a plank of wood.

The Inside-Out Teacher

She wore her jumper inside-out –
we could all see the seams,
it had to stay the whole day long
or she would not see her dreams.

She wore her belt the wrong way round,
with the buckle at the back,
sitting on an upright chair
it gave her back a crack.

She wore her smile upside-down,
to make the children giggle,
they ran off to the playground
with a wriggle and a wiggle.

The Ballet Teacher

She walks on a bottomless duvet,
her arms carve arcs in the air –

fingers outstretched,
boat-bottom hands,

they fall like feathers
never reaching the ground.

Her circle skirt pleats
glide behind her, beside her,

folding, unfolding –
an opening fan.

Her voice glances each child
with gossamer.

Bubble Gun Paradiddle

pull the trigger   bubble up
pull the trigger   bubble down
pull the trigger   pull the trigger
bubbles   getting   awful   bigger,
pull   the   trigger   turning   round,
standing   in   your   dressing   gown.

A paradiddle is a drumming pattern.

Punctuate That Lunch You Ate

Punctuate that lunch you ate
last Thursday in the caff,

those beans would like a comma
and those sausages a dash.

Not to mention that the egg
wants a curly question mark,

and if the chips don't get one too
they'll get in a terrible nark.

The tomatoes want quotation marks,
the mushrooms are on the hop –

because all they want to see
is a brown sauce squirt full stop.

Me, Myself, I

You are a very important person,
You always have a CAPITAL 'I',
You are a very important person,
I speak no word of a lie,
You are a very important person,
Whether you're a cool girl or a gorgeous guy,
You're a very important person,
You deserve a CAPITAL 'I'.

In fact, without a doubt,
You deserve a CAPITAL 'I'
Which climbs straight through the ceiling
And hits the clear blue sky
Where a dragonfly is singing,
"Can I have a CAPITAL 'I'?"

TOP TABLE

(A found poem)

Yr1
LILLY – making up a new game in the playground

REUBEN – talking to his seeds to make them grow

Yr2
ABDULA – eating every bit of his lunch for a whole week

RAHSAAN – putting away equipment in the stripy box

Yr 3
TYLER – always being friendly to everyone in his class

BUNTARIG – being a great football team player

Yr 4
MERWISH – listening so hard that her ears fell off

HUZAIGA – playing with the younger children outside

Yr 5
ADEELA – being someone everyone wants to be like

WAJIHA – smiling through it all

Yr 6
MUSTJAB – trying to make friends and join in

DARIUS – helping to put all the animal books in the
library into alphabetical order

Lou's Pyjama-Uniform

It was cold when Lou got ready for bed,
it was warm in her school uniform,
she couldn't see the point of taking it off
to shiver in her bed till dawn.

So she pulled her nightie over the top
and climbed into her bed,
her mum was gone to work by seven,
so nothing was ever said.

Until one day her headteacher
dragged Lou into her room.
"Why is your uniform so crumpled,
do you not have an iron at home?"

"We do have an iron," said Lou in defence,
"but it's cold at home in my room,
so I sleep inside my uniform."
Lou let out a huge wide yawn.

"Doesn't your mother tell you off?"
"Oh no, she sees my nightie.
I put it on over the top,
then pray to the Almighty."

Lou's mum was phoned straight away,
she came into school for a meeting.
Lou now has a new smooth uniform,
and her house has central heating.

Kassandra

Kassandra is my silent friend,
she doesn't know how to speak,
she smiles and sticks her tongue out
and dances down the street.

Her hair is spun like candy floss,
her skin is ivory white,
she runs across the playground,
jumping like a kite.

The other day I asked her,
if she had a wish or three,
What would she want?
What would she wish?
What would she want to be?

She stood there in amazement,
she spun around three times,
she came to a halt,
knelt down on the ground
and drew pictures in the sand.

First she drew a wide sun,
its rays long and strong,
then she drew a reindeer
dragging a sledge along.

Then she drew a lily,
its petals curved and sleek,
then she drew a mountain
with a tall spiky peak.

Last she drew a little girl
standing by a tree,
she pointed at the little girl,
then pointed straight at me.

The Ice Man

He slid into our classroom –
a six-foot man in a block of ice.
Cool, or what?
We stood him near the radiator –
a pool of water spread across the floor.

The tip of his nose,
the back of his hands,
then his shoulders began to show.
The water lapped around our feet.

Mark went home to get his swimming gear,
Sureya made a fleet of boats,
Esther floated up to the window.
Our teacher gave up on the Egyptians
and blew up a lilo.

Just before the water reached the top of the door
the Ice Man began to drink,
he slurped and gulped and swallowed and gurgled
until the room was completely dry.
His mouth unfroze to a smile,
his chest heaved with a sigh,
then he left the room as silently as he'd arrived.

There is a damp patch where he stood
which never quite goes away.

Roundabout

I'm sitting still
on the roundabout,
the trees are all a blur,

the slide and swings
spin into one,
I can hear a gentle whirr.

The clouds are rushing
through the sky,
like pillows on a stick.

Two boys
are playing football.
Kick, kick, kick.

The ice cream van
comes round three times.
Which flavour would I choose?

A strawberry cone?
A Ninety-Nine?
Or a lolly made from juice?

Two girls
are on the climbing frame,
they've nearly reached the top.

I've been spinning,
spinning, spinning round.
My head says it's time to stop!

I Like the Taste of Computers

For Oldfield Park Infants, Bath

I like the taste of computers,
I like the feel of the sky,
I like the sound of potatoes,
I like the look of a sigh.

I like the smell of windows,
the feel of a wide rainbow,
I like the taste of winter,
and the sound of thick deep snow.

How to Make a Cup of Tea

again for William Patten School, Stoke Newington

Take the mouse out of the teapot.
Pour in two cupfuls of ice.

Boil the kettle and leave the water to cool.
Find some tea.
This could be elephant and magnet tea,
hundreds and thousands tea,
or – the always popular – bag of nails tea.

Shovel the tea into the pot.
Don't bother pouring out the iced water –
it will mingle nicely with the cool water from the kettle.
Pour the water from the kettle steadily into the teapot.
Leave it for half an hour to settle down and stop giggling.

Find six teacups. Six is always a good number.
Don't worry about the saucers.
Never make the mistake of asking if anyone takes sugar.
If they say 'Yes' and you've run out,
then you'll have to go out and buy some.

Milk the cat.

The Noodle Eater

I am a noodle eater,
I eat them in the night,
I eat them by the basketful
and give my dad a fright.

I eat them dry,
I eat them wet,
I eat them upside-down.
And best of all I eat them with –
an eyebrow-meeting-frown.

Food Sense

What I like about the smell of food is
chicken roasting in the oven.

What I like about the sound of food is
onions frying in a pan.

What I like about the feel of food is
a shiny apple in my hand.

What I like about the look of food is
strawberries, raspberries and blueberries piled high in my
bowl.

What I like about the taste of food is
popping popcorn,
tingly ice cream,
salty chips,
crunchy carrots,
slimy yoghurt,
wobbly jelly,
and long long strands of slippy slurpy spaghetti.

Boxes at Chapel Street Market

For Winton Primary School, King's Cross

Cheery tomatoes,
cherry tomatoes,
smiling to each other,
reflecting the sun in their
redness.

Hairy coconuts,
hairy coconuts,
a nose, and two eyes
looking out
at the crowd.

Bitter melon,
bitter melon,
green and spiky
scary hedgehogs
hooking up together.

Pak choi, pak choi,
packed tight
snuggling up till
they stir for a fry.

Ginger, ginger, ginger,
knobbly, like finger joints,
ready to flavour soup.

Oranges, oranges
piled high from heated Egypt,
their dimply skin ripe
for your thumb.

The Pointlessness of Not Buying Your Own Strawberry Ice Cream

"Can I have a lick?"
"No."

"Can I have a bite?"
"No."

"Can I have the end with a bit of ice-cream on it?"
"No."

"Well can I have a lick then?"
"No!"

Summer Pudding

for Carol

The pudding of summer
bursts on my tongue
like the glisten of sun on the sea.

The grit of the seeds is the sand
in my toes, and the sand
which sticks to my knee.

The red of the juice
is the blood on my leg
when I fell on a stone on the shore.

In the sharp days of winter
I'll remember the berries,
the running and splashing,

the skimming and swimming,
wanting more and more and more.

Making Cream Cakes
for Tina Turner

It was a dream I had last week.
She phoned to say the paper got it wrong –
'If you want to look good, you have to
care about yourself, eat brown rice,
steamed vegetables, and dance.'

In fact she adores pavlova and crème brûlée,
she'd die for trifle with real custard,
nothing beats a blackcurrant tart
crusted with caster sugar.

Her absolute favourites are a mousse
so full of chocolate that the spoon stands up,
and a rhubarb crumble gone rock solid the next day.

Propagating Thyme

I'm propagating Thyme –
from now on there will be more Tuesdays,
and a proliferation of Sage
every other Thursday.

Rosemary will bring
a thirteenth month
whenever she visits on Sunday.

Parsley is nurturing
recurring months –
March, April, May.

Wish Sandwich

Between two slices of
    the Caspian Sea
  I'd like a yellow lilo

        Inside a
  crunchy cedar bun
  I'd like high season
        in the sun

Call it a wrap
with a whale
inside and
clouds of
minnows
on the
side

        Last
    of all I'd like
  a roll with a feather
    filling for my
        soul

Government Health Warning

Don't squash peas on your knees,
Don't grate carrot on a parrot,
Don't tangle pears in your nostril hairs
Never risk a quid on a squid.

Don't pour bottled beer in your ear.
Never slice apple pies on your thighs.
Never wash your pullovers with yesterday's leftovers.
Don't entice a bowl of egg fried rice.

Don't assume that tarragon's a paragon,
Or try to run faster than a bag of spinach pasta,
Don't try a lunge at Victoria sponge,
A cake with a steak is a mistake.

Bravado never works with avocado,
A flickin's not the thing to give to chicken,
Don't go and stutter on the b-b-b-b-butter
Never feed mice on ice.

Careful not to ravage a coy Savoy cabbage,
Never have a tussle with a mussel,
Don't ever hurry with a spicy prawn curry,
Don't boast about your buttered toast.

Don't pour jelly in your welly,
Don't dribble tagliatelle on your older brother's belly.
Never do the tango with a ripe and juicy mango,
If you do then you're sure to pay the price!

Files Not Found on a Computer

The Touch File

a son stroking his father's cheek,
fingers folding a hamster's fur,
a face buried in cherry blossom,
enclosing arms of goodnight.

The Taste File

the saltiness of boiled ham
against soft white bread,
the sharpness of marmalade
melding with butter on wholemeal toast,
the twang of rhubarb and ginger
hiding beneath crunchy crumble,
the cut of iced sparkling water
swilling down my throat.

The Aroma File

a wet dog in the rain,
garlic squashed beneath a knife,
lavender steaming from my bath,
croissant warming Sunday morning.

The Listening Station

It hears the wind that rushes through the trees
saying something of the sea,
it hears a moth leaving the ceiling,
it hears the thin pages of a book close,
it hears a late key turn in the door.

It hears an egg flop into a mixing bowl,
it hears the crack of a bended knee,
it hears a wash leather squeak down a window pane,
it hears an apple eaten to its rotten core.

It hears a pencil dragged across tissue paper,
it hears a pea-stick snapped in half,
it hears a mouth leave another mouth,
it hears a lion (or is it a child?) roar.

A Slew of Clerihew

Tutankhamun

Tutankhamun
Died too soon,
He lay in the Valley of Kings
Surrounded by golden things.

Queen Victoria

Queen Victoria
Was bursting with euphoria
When Prince Albert's ambition
Produced the Great Exhibition.

Henry VIII

Henry the Eight
Had very bad breath,
That's why every wife
Had a very short life.

William Shakespeare

William Shakespeare
Showed no fear,
He killed off his leading men
So they couldn't come back again.

The Hysterical Tulip

(to be read at the top of your voice in an open space whilst shaking your head)

I have red and white stripes AND I'm a tulip!
I have red and white stripes AND I'm a tulip!
I have red and white stripes AND I'm a tulip!
I have red and white stripes AND I'm a tulip!

Death in the Poetry Library

He stood between the stacks,
fishing out his reference.
Two flippant boys appeared,
paid little heed to the sign
'Please check aisle before ....',
they wheeled the shelves together.
The poet, squashed between
authors L to M, wheezed.
Released, he lumbered
to the floor.

There was no blood.
His lines of verse
lapped along the corridor.

Messages from the Heart Scarab to the Heart

Don't tell I stole from my mum's purse to buy the latest
Jacqueline Wilson,
don't tell I ran in front of a car to avoid Barry Smith,
don't tell I stitched an aeroplane to the sky.

Don't tell I ate a whole bag of Thornton's
Continental Chocolates from my auntie's cupboard,
don't tell I took a razor to lift the soles of the shoes
I was supposed to shine.

Don't tell I cut the string on my daddy's garden chimes,
don't tell I put a dustbin through the science lab window,
don't tell I touched the curlew's egg.

'The Heart Scarab was an essential Egyptian funerary amulet placed over the heart. On the underside a spell is inscribed telling the heart to say nothing during the Weighing of the Heart ceremony for fear that it might make a guilty confession.' Horniman Museum.

The British Museum Print Room

Van Gogh thought to be a preacher.
At twenty-one he came here and saw
the Rembrandt brown ink drawing over there,
then he did his own.

It lies in this glass case –
a splutter of rocks in the foreground,
a scruff of grass.
He drew every tree one behind the other
pulling right back to the horizon.

Dots become finer,
fields become thinner,
a track ripples to the right
while a train drags smoke to the left.

Stooks measure fields,
cypresses billow,
nothing is still.

Figure

When I arrived Suilven
wore a scarf of cloud

across her shoulder.
Next day, pouting at Canisp,

a chestnut beret at half cock.
Her skirts were low

with mist on Thursday.
Today, her shape,

with sun, is kissed.

Suilven and Canisp are mountains in the Highlands of Scotland.

When I Travelled from the Country to the City

for Carol

When I travelled from the country to the city
the wind remained in my veins,

the heather spread through my fingers,
the moor sprawled over my back.

The quilted hillside was heavy
when I lay beneath it to rest,

my dreams were of rivers and valleys,
of a sky streaming east to west.

Benches, Tresco

They're placed at considerate intervals –
curved hurricane pine,
some weathered and scored,

some lichened and worn,
some with holes
where the trunk swallowed a branch.

From a bench I saw a blackbird with an orange beak,
the promise of protea in fat downy buds,
the chequerboard bark of an endless palm.

From a bench I saw wagtails surrounding a horse,
the stripes of shelduck tipped up in a lake,
the oblique flight of pheasants.

From a bench I saw Atlantic waves
drawing breath, raising their shoulders
and spewing their seething froth right back to the shore.

From a bench I saw an insect in flight,
the blades of its wings whirred away from the island,
it carried me back to rumbling ground.

Limerick 1

There was a young boy from Peru,
who never knew quite what to do.
He rubbed his nose
and wriggled his toes,
then painted his village bright blue.

Limerick 2

There was a young man from Capri,
who had a very sore knee,
he slathered it in balm
and ruptured his arm,
and ran home to drink cups of tea

(with sugar)

NYNY

Beware,
    I
    have
    New York
    in my eyes.
 Balconies with a
closed lid of snow,
two poached eggs in
a cup, the flash of
static as my finger
hits the Chrysler tower.
A lift flying eighty
floors in less than
a minute, a lift
which never comes,
an unflushable toilet,
a toilet which
flushes when I open
the door. A window
from my room looks
into an opposite room –
a woman wears
antennae to watch
TV. A tall man with
wide Halloween hair,
black lenses in his
eyes, bends low to
kiss his small pale
girlfriend on the
forehead. The snow
is stacked in mountain
ranges at the end of
each sidewalk.
Care is needed to get
across to the other side.

78

Night Sky in the Clun Valley

for Vincent

The sky is throwing out woks,
The moon is munching bananas,
The stars wear sparkly socks,
The planets are harbouring llamas.

World Secrets

The people of Hungary have huge appetites,
Romania has no space at all,
Newfoundland has yet to be discovered,
In Trinidad the fathers have a ball.

You won't find a telegraph wire in Poland,
Armenia is full of generous souls,
In Russia the men walk slowly,
The houses in Andorra don't have doors.

In Finland no one eats fish,
Minnows are eaten by Wales,
In Turkey they prefer chicken,
In Sardinia, a piece of toast never fails.

In Germany all children are squeaky clean,
In Greece they cook with olive oil,
In Cuba the people are very round,
Iceland is a country always on the boil.

Chile is the place for jumpers,
In Korea everyone gets ahead,
In Jersey they wear cardigans,
In Kuwait they've given up

and
    gone
        home
            to
                bed.

Krakatoa Meets Popocateptl

If Krakatoa could slide into the Indian Ocean,
fly over Angola,
sail the Atlantic,
glide into the Gulf of Mexico –
it could exchange pumice and gas
with Popocateptl.

Or, Popocateptl could
dive into the Pacific,
bypass Papua New Guinea,
slip between Java and Sumatra
and lavish ash and lava
on crackling Krakatoa.

As it is they stay exactly where they are,
keeping an eye out for each other's
belching smoke, spewing jets of fire;
keeping an ear out for an explosion
louder than an atom bomb;
and watching the stars,

which sometimes, not wanting to be left out,
throw silver-plated meteors at them.

River Torridge

I knew the river hid
behind the bank,
lying, like a length of silk,
stretched between the willows.

The surface ripped,
something dived –
gone too long to be a bird.

Weasel head above the water,
down he went again,
a flash of oily fur.

He swam up beside,
this time he stayed,
looking at me straight.
I walked to keep his pace.

I loved his length –
his tail his body,
his body his tail,
his tail the river's length.
We moved together
through the wind,
along the river's course.

Another dive,
I skimmed the current,
searching for his guise.

He'd gone on alone.
I felt him though,
gliding through
the river's strength.

Moon Jelly Fish, Horniman Museum

Handkerchiefs of jelly fish
flex across azure blue,
sculling up the tank
like fragile umbrellas
bowed against a storm.

Pulsing downwards,
followed by clouds of ribbon legs,
their mushroom rims
fold open, fold closed.

Hung with a string of fibre optics
they turn inside-out, ragged,
hovering next to each other
to puzzle over the lack of shore.

The Humpback's Wail

For Gothic Mede Lower School, Arlesey

For twenty hours I sing my song,
my body arched, my head hung down.
I sing for her to come along
and swim up close beside me.

She'll love my sound,
my clicks and squeaks,
my lilting moans,
my squeals and creaks.

She'll immediately appreciate
the trouble I take
to vary my song
as it flows through the deep.

Barnacled like me,
she'll have lumps and bumps,
a slip-slapping tail
and a wild beauty.

We'll stay in warm waters
while our baby is born.
Come to me soon,
don't leave me lovelorn.

The Very Fortunate Frog

I live in a rubber tub,
it's a very fancy home,
my ceiling's made of lily pads,
I really cannot moan.

At night I go for a wander,
slurp up a worm or two,
flick on a fly, and wonder why,
some frogs live in a zoo.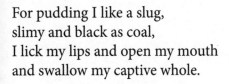

For pudding I like a slug,
slimy and black as coal,
I lick my lips and open my mouth
and swallow my captive whole.

I plan on living for forty years,
squelching in the mud,
basking in the morning sun,
if I could dance a jig I would.

On hot days in July,
when I'm feeling sleepy-snoozie,
a hose pipe fills my fancy home,
and turns it into a jacuzzi.

The Two-Toed Sloth's Boast

I may be a two-toed sloth,
but you should see me move,
I can run faster than a garden snail,
my fur is green and smooth.

I go to the toilet once a week,
I never need a drink,
I suck the moisture from my food –
it leaves me time to think.

What Do You Suppose?

If I get up in the morning
and find a shoe on the lawn,
a shoe on the patio,
a sandal in a flower pot –
what do you suppose?

If I take them inside
and find another shoe is missing
and I find that shoe
upside-down in a freshly dug hole –
what do you suppose?

That I left the back door open by mistake?
That while I was sleeping a fox crept in?
That she giggled loudly as she passed my door?

Did she peep at me sleeping?
Did she hear my sonorous snore?

Wasp on the Tube

If I knew how I got here
I wouldn't have commmmmmmmmme,

those doors banged shut,
that was the end of my funnnnnnnnnnnn,

I'm buzzing around
and causing a hummmmmmmmmmmm,

they're all looking up
and they think I am dummmmmmmmmb.

I want to escape,
get back to the sunnnnnnnnnnnnnnnnnnn,

that boy's going mad
and grabbing his mummmmmmmmmmm,

if we weren't in a tunnel
I know they'd all runnnnnnnnnnnnnnnnnn,

at last, King's Cross,
my tube journey's donnnnnnnnnnnnnnne.

Birds I

a murmuration of starlings
became
a clattering of choughs

a quarrel of sparrows
gave way to
a squabble of seagulls

despite
a scolding of jays
what followed was
a murder of crows

Grey Heron, Crystal Palace Dinosaur Park

Broken black streaks
feather his throat,

black eyebrows shoot
into a Mandarin's moustache.

Eyes staring ahead,
rigid as the cement pterodactyl

in flight to his right,
head darts down.

He straightens with a fish in his beak,
slowly gulping,

like sucking
on a saved caramel.

The Night Flight of the Pterodactyl

As I wait for the right current of air
a moonbeam glistens on my claw.

I take off from the highest mountain –
not without grace,
not without speed,
and with a spine of pride
which tingles to my gleaming teeth –
I'm the largest creature to fly.

Gliding over the lake I make
a black shadow with my shape,
warm blood pumps through my jaw.

I swoop on a sleeping frog,
look up at the swarming stars,
then end his dream with a snap.

Cormorant

You'll know me from my hooked beak,
my beady eyes, the way I hang my wings
to dry. I stand on a post in the lake,
relish the breeze rustling my feathers.

You'd think my wings were waterproof –
I spend so much time submerged,
but I rather like hanging around
after a surge through waves and rain.

I can ponder the state of the nation,
watch walkers walking their mutts.
If I didn't have this quiet time,
I'd go completely nuts!

Flamingo Blumingo

Flamingos are gregarious birds,
they rarely stand alone,
twenty thousand in one place,
not one allowed to moan.

For if they started –
"My leg is aching,"
"A bone's stuck in my U-bend neck,"
they'd drive each other flamingo crazy,
so they just say, "Flipping heck!"

Jamie the Jumpling

Have you any idea how scared I am?
I'm three weeks old, I've no feathers,
and I'm supposed to fly?
This cliff edge has been my home,
now it's the launch pad
to the rest of my life!
I've been standing here
for two hours now.
My mum can nudge me
as much as she likes,
I am NOT jumping into that sea!
It's miles away!
She keeps telling me it's 'do or die',
I either take the leap
or I'm lunch for a herring gull.
Well I'm going nowhere!
If only I had a brother
or a sister, but no,
guillemot policy is one child only.
Dad says when we land
we will swim to Norway.
That's two hundred miles away!
What does he think I am –
a cruise ship?
Everyone is jumping now,
I'm the only one left,
I don't want to stay here by myself.
Maybe I'll take a tiny step
towards the edge.
That's not too bad.
I'll take another.

Perhaps if I close my eyes
and wait for a breeze?
Oh well, here goes,
North Sea here I
C
  O
    M
     M
      M
       M
        M
         M
          M
           M
            M
             M
              M
               M
                M
                 M
                  M
                   M
                    M
                     M
                      M
                       M
                        M
                         M
                         E
                        !

Birds II

a bouquet of pheasants
was given to
a charm of finches

a wisp of snipe
spooled over
a ballet of swans

a rafter of turkeys
bumped into
a herd of wrens

a paddling of ducks
was drowned by
a descent of woodpeckers

a deceit of lapwings
recognized
an unkindness of ravens

a siege of herons
superseded
a dread of terns

a vein of goldfinches
was sold in
a bazaar of guillemots

a convocation of eagles
winked at
a stare of owls

The Solar-Powered Fairy

for Celia

I'm a solar-powered fairy,
I'm dependent on the light,
if the sun is shining daily,
then I twinkle in the night.

If the day is dull and dreary,
my wings flop all about,
my smile turns down,
I lose my crown,
my head is full of doubt.

A sunny day in winter
is when I'm at my best,
I soak up the rays
and think of ways
of filling you with zest.

I flutter through the evergreens,
spread sparkle on your lawn,
I'm in each dewdrop shining
on the blades of grass at dawn.

I scintillate the snow
which lies outside your door,
I light your way,
lift up your day – hey-hey!

Then I pirouette, and fly away.

Teddy Balloon

I blew up my balloon with helium
and let go of the string.
It flew above my garden,
bob-bobbing in the wind.

It flew above the houses,
above a chimney pot,
it flew along with seagulls
till it was a tiny dot.

It cleared the misty mountains,
dissolved into a cloud,
"Come back, my bouncy Teddy,
Come back," I cried out loud.

But Teddy's gone forever,
away over the sea.
Now I know that I can cry,
but he won't come back to me.

Dusk at the Botanical Gardens, Bath

Magnolia buds stand proud of their stems
like the tips of cats' tails,
crocus close their cups.

A papaya sun pushes down on the roofs,
the moon is half a melting pancake.

Postcard from the Bathroom

I'm on holiday in my bathroom,
the sun is streaming in,
the air lock in the water pipes
makes an awful din.

I'm lying in hot water
with ice cream down my chin,
racing my clockwork terrapins –
I know which one will win.

Mum's making tuna sandwiches
with bread cut really thin,
she hands them on a plastic plate
with a cheeky seaside grin.

It's better than Ibiza,
no queuing for check-in,
just lie back in my steamy pool,
rivers in my skin.

A Beach for Ruksar

This beach has blonde sand sieved as fine as flour,
pebbles in sixteen shades of blue,
smooth black rock which shines with every tide.

Lines of limpets shelter in the cracks,
a pool appears with waving crabs and swaying weed.
There's bladder wrack and razor shells,
and waves which rise and crash
and bubble to the shore.

At first the sea feels icy cold,
you scream and run away.
"Come back Ruksar," it says to you,
"Try again, be bold."

You teeter on the edge a while
then stretch your arms and launch into the surf.
Your eyes are bright,
you smile out loud,
your body shakes with a watery laugh.

Mike's Mountain Barbeque

On Monday a midwife toad
jumps through raindrops from the hermitage
to watch Mike barbeque –
a green gingham oven glove.

On Tuesday three yellow butterflies
with clouded judgment get a lift on a snowflake
to watch Mike barbeque –
the pig bin.

On Wednesday five underprivileged crickets
fly on the wind from the San Pedro valley
to watch Mike barbeque –
a lifetime's supply of chewing gum.

On Thursday eleven wasps from the post box
ignore the thunder
to watch Mike barbeque –
the neighbour's washing line.

On Friday fourteen roe deer
spring from the sunshine in a nearby field
to watch Mike barbeque –
a three-legged clog.

On Saturday seventeen gruff griffon vultures
drop in from Dobres, not a care for the frost,
to watch Mike barbeque –
two Golden Jubilee balloons.

On Sunday Mike ski jumps
over the cable car at Fuente Dé.
The pressure is low, the sky is clear,
the snow is as firm as a boned leg of lamb.

Bradshaw Plots his Revenge

As if being sunk in a bowl of soapy water wasn't enough,
now I'm pegged by my left ear
between blue shorts
and a pair of jogging bottoms.

I'm dry to my nose,
my legs are sodden,
and I'm dripping from my woolly toes.

I must hang here while they go
climbing castles,
skimming stones,
poking jellyfish.
Then I'm expected to listen to their adventures
when they get home!

Well I won't!
I will shut my ears,
purse my lips
and clench my fists.
They won't know the difference.

Limpet

I am a Cornish limpet,
 been here for a hundred years,
    sucking and gripping and sticking to this stone
     with a hundred thousand fears.

     What if I get put in a bucket
        and dumped in the boot of a car,
           with wellies and jellies and a windbreaker
            and a shell in the shape of a star?

        I'd miss my chats with the ancient crab,
          the swell and wash of the tide,
            the soothing stroke of anemones,
              the storms when the fish come and hide.

          But I hang on tight and hope for the best,
            I avoid anyone with a spade,
              when the sun beats down in a glisten on the sea,
               my fears begin to fade.

The Return of the Wildman of Orford

Was I a wildman or was I a merman?
Did I have whiskers or was it a tail?
None of this matters, since 1167
I've learnt to be strong,
as strong as a whale.

Back then I was caught
in nets with the fishes,
I floundered with flounder,
was mocked by a haddock,
I laughed at the soul of a Dover sole.

Strung up by my feet
you questioned my silence.
I ask you – how could I speak
of the deep to those who don't know
that the sea is darker than a December night,
that the sea is deeper than amethyst,
that the sea can wrap you in an iron clasp,
that the sea can whisper, and the sea can rasp?

You let me swim between lines of nets,
I dipped and dived and found my way free.
For eight hundred years I've soared the waves,
never been caught, been allowed to be.

I'm back to tell you I'm neither
merman nor monster,
nor a fiend nor a ghoul.
I'm the spirit of the sea.
And I'm nobody's fool.

The Merman of Orford is said to have appeared in or around 1167.

The Fragrant Pirate

For Westcott First School near Dorking

You can't let your standards slip on ship,
there may be rats and a bilge water stench,
but I take care to always indulge
in a little late night pampering.

The sun and wind play havoc with my skin,
so when the lights go dim at eight
I smooth my face with a very large tin
of soothing yellow lanolin.

As the hulk creaks and my shipmates snore,
we rock and roll with the waves.
I rub my feet with jasmine oil,
just as my fourteenth wife did on shore.

Lavender and musk are a must
to inhale after hours of smoke from cannons,
I pour three drops on my sack of a pillow –
sound sleep will surely follow?

Lanolin is a fatty substance found on sheep's wool which is used in
moisturizer

Piccalilli and Bottle Top

Piccalilli is a yellow child
with an onion for her head.
Her legs are stalks of cauliflower,
she lies on a mustard bed.

You can't mistake Bottle Top,
for whenever he is near,
a distinctive rattle, clink-clonk-click
is all that you will hear.

Bottle Top and Piccalilli
are truly best of friends.
If he rattles on, or she gets too sour,
they always make amends.

One day they went to the seaside,
a man spotted Lill on the sands,
he shoved her inside his sandwich
with his great big pork pie hands.

B.T. was quick into action,
he danced on Pork Pie's head,
his eyes rolled around at the awful sound
and his face went Ribena red.

Lill slipped away to the ocean,
Bottle Top was soon on her tail,
they had a very nice day at Westgate Bay –
Pork Pie was squashed by a whale.

Riddle

It's a boat in the air,
it swings and it rocks.
it carries a pair of glasses,
two books, a pair of holey socks.

It's stripy and it's dappled,
it lies in dark and shade,
it's a place to float away,
to forget the existence of clocks.

The answer to this riddle is somewhere in this book!

The Powder Monkey

This is the moment I dread,
my eyes sting with smoke,
my ears sing with cannon fire.
I see the terror rise inside me,
coil a rope in my belly to keep it down.
I chant inside my head to freeze my nerve.

Main mast, mizzen mast, foremast,
belfry, capstan, waist.

We must keep the fire coming.
If I dodge the sparks
my cartridge will be safe,
if I learn my lessons
I can be a seaman,
if I close my eyes to eat my biscuit
I will not see the weevils.

Main mast, mizzen mast, foremast,
shock lockers, bowsprit, gripe.

Don't stop to put out that fire,
run to the hold,
we must fire at them
or they will fire at us.

Main mast, mizzen mast, foremast,
belfry, capstan, waist.

My mother never knew me,
but she would want to know this –
I can keep a cannon going,
I do not need her kiss.

Before 1794 children aged 6 upward went to sea. After 1794 the minimum age was 13.

Isopod Song

for George and Can

I so wanted to be an ipod,
play tunes at the bottom of the sea,
tap my fourteen feet in time,
bounce my baby on my knee.

It would help to lift the gloom
among the sea cucumbers and sponges,
instead we nibble on a whale
and stretch our sixteen inches.

I try to sing a famous song,
but really it's not the same;
at the bottom of the sea
it's hard to make your name.

But when shoals of fish
swim by and give a friendly nod,
I think maybe it's not so bad
to be a giant isopod.

Lifeline

Your clothes still smell of cinnamon and garlic,
your hand of lavender and musk,

despite the drenching and the soaking,
the days you must have floated

between stern and sodden deck.
Chesil's arm of pebbles beckoned,

guided you to Wyke,
and here you lie, who are you?

with stained glass blue all round you
bringing your dead eyes alight.

You've knotted wrack and thong-weed
plaited through your hair,

I'll pick it out and keep it,
lay these lilies at your feet,

bring flowers to you daily,
be your sister while you need me,

sweep the aisle, wipe the altar,
I'll see you claimed, all right.

Your lips are grey as lias,
your fingers hold the air,

your bones are made from beauty,
when I touch your arm, you care.

*Mary Anning (palaeontologist and fossil hunter) visited the body of a
woman washed ashore in 1815 after the* Alexander *sailing ship was
wrecked off the Dorset coast.*

Playground in the Rain

The tractor does not wobble on its spring,
the slide is not slid upon,
the helter skelter makes a solitary swirl,
the swings cannot remember when the sun last shone.

The benches wait for watching parents,
the dustbin's tummy rumbles,
the climbing frame train is going nowhere,
the roundabout grumbles over its soaking chairs.

Wet

Wet letters through the letter box,
an orchestration of drips,
delphiniums bent with weight of water,
street party calls it quits.

Rain in Nice

My disdain for the rain on the Côte d'Azur
lasted only as long as the drizzle.
Grasping strength, it pelted the leaves
of lemon trees, skimmed the skins of olives,
laid boughs of bougainvillaea low.

The fronds of palms trees dribbled,
umbrella palms dripped,
oleander blooms drooped,
the veil of rain thickened.

Then, still.

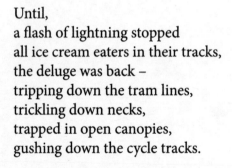

Until,
a flash of lightning stopped
all ice cream eaters in their tracks,
the deluge was back –
tripping down the tram lines,
trickling down necks,
trapped in open canopies,
gushing down the cycle tracks.

In its wake –
a blush of petals on the glossy pavement,
a sea restored to cerulean,
keen air, fresh enough to breathe.

Gales of Laughter

ha   ho   teehee
   ha   ho   teehee
      ha   ho   teehee
        ha   ho   teehee
       ha   ho   teehee
      ha   ho   teehee
     ha   ho   teehee
     ha
    ha   ho
  ha   ho
ha   ho
        hee
  teeheehee   hee
            hee
    teeheehee   hee
             hee
     teeheehee   hee
             hee
   teeheehee   hee
          hee
  teeheehee   hee
         hee
teehee   hee
       hee
     hee
   hee
  hee

Walter the Water Wizard

If you have a headache
I swim up the tap
and add a little aspirin
to give that pain a zap.

When you're in the shower
and you run out of gel,
I wriggle up the showerhead
and squirt a dreamy smell.

If you're in the swimming pool
convinced you're going to sink,
I'm standing underneath you –
floating's easier than you think.

My favourite though is making snow
from the dampness in the sky,
every flake is different –
they land on your hand with a sigh.

Swimming at Forest Hill

There's one who walks across the pool,
and two who natter at the side,
another shivers at the shallow end
standing half in half out.

Below the glass surface a swimsuit skirt
billows like a sea anemone.
The talking pair take a swim across, together,
but only when the way is clear,

they're scuppered when a shark dives in
with sleek black skin and goggles –
they know she'll do super-crawl, never looking up.
The walking woman tries a doggy paddle,

holds up her head and scampers for her life.
When her paw touches the far side
we all stop dead.
And slap our dripping flippers.

The Roman Baths

I threw a coin into the sacred pool
and made a secret wish.

If I tell the wish
then I will never have a friend,

If I tell the wish
then wars will never end,

If I tell the wish
my angel fish might die,

If I tell the wish
I will always wonder why

I threw a stone in the sacred pool
and made a secret wish.

Mountain Biker Poster

I used to jump the pavement,
do wheelies in the air,
but now I'm in a photograph
and I just sit and stare.

My feet won't touch the tarmac,
the handle-bars are turned,
my gloves have melted on my hands
and my nose is rather burned.

Back to School

The smell of mincemeat
on the stairs,

a queue of Year 2 waiting
to be shot by flashbulbs,

the stack and curve of
grey plastic chairs,

a gold bell chiming
the end of play-time,

pencil shavings curling
down the throat of the bin.

Freya's New Pair of Shoes

Freya's feet were very small,
in fact she usually wore tied-up leaves,
but since it was nearly winter,
she bought herself some shoes.

The shoes were black, the shoes were shiny,
they strapped across her feet,
the heels were strong and clicked along,
the buckles very neat.

When she put them on and sang a song
she rose up in the air,
feet first she flew with a swishing sound
followed by her hair.

She landed on a treetop,
overlooking a glistening lake,
when she flew again she landed
in her best friend's birthday cake.

A third flight proved quite dangerous,
she flew right across the sea
and landed in a fishing boat,
on the fisherman's knobbly knee.

By this time she was exhausted,
it was nearly time to sleep,
so she flew right under her duvet,
where her dozy sleep was deep.

Iris Upsidaisy

Iris Upsidaisy has corkscrew curls,
they're corn-yellow spinning coils,
they twist and they whirl.

They twist around the library,
they twist along the street,
they twirl up lamp posts
and round the shoppers' feet.

They whirl along telegraph wires
and up the traffic lights,
they curl around chestnut trees
on cold and windy nights.

They spin along her forehead,
they bounce up and down,
they shake when she laughs out loud,
they hide a puzzled frown.

When her curls are resting
on her pillow while she sleeps,
they straighten out and stretch themselves
then lie around in heaps.

Iris wakes in the morning
and her curls curl up again,
they dance with glee for all to see –
her jitterbugging mane!

The jitterbug: a fast dance performed to swing music, popular in the 1940s

The Year is Turning

Gulls chance the churning sea,
    Leaves stack up against the thermal door,
Tips of willows, russet, finger low grey sky,
    The year is drawing in.

Old man's beard billows by the road,
    A net of mist hangs over Swanbourne Lake,
Rosehips thrust from scratchy hedgerows,
    The year is turning in.

Elastic Band Boy

Elastic Band
Boy collects
elastic bands,
he spins after
postmen, picks
up their throw-
aways then
threads them
down the stem
of his scooter.
He has over
three hundred
bands threaded
on his scooter.
He's thinking
of melting
them down
and making
them into a
huge tyre to put
on his bicycle.
When he gets one.

The Shortest Days

for Suze

How dark is the morning,
how dark is the day,
will the sun shoulder
the darkness away?

The cars shine their headlights
at lunch-time,
the dawn stays the same
until dusk, snow sits –
tall hats on the seedheads,
an afternoon dew takes a rest.

How dark is the evening,
how dark is the day,
will the sun soon
shiver the darkness away?

The Rugby Tournament

At the end of the last match of the season
there were four front teeth

poking out of the pitch,
two players had one arm each in a sling,

and there were possibly three little toes broken –
all on left feet.

Five sets of parents were hoarse from shouting
and couldn't go to work the next day.

Seven grans had hypothermia,
despite being wrapped in twelve tartan rugs.

Three little sisters have very snotty colds.
Everybody is dying for the next season to begin.

The Girl Who Lives Under a Stone

She doesn't know the World Cup has started,
that Ginger Spice has left The Girls,
that Barbie Doll has got a boyfriend,
that bootlegs are the pair of pants to wear in town.

She knows her ants from her woodlice,
she knows when a frost has hit the ground,
she knows that moss shines lime in moonlight,
she knows that moths don't leave a sound.

Planet Nothing

I kneel up on our high-backed chair,
stretch my arms towards the sky,
pull the lever on the arm,
and at precisely a quarter to three
I am shot into the air.

Lakes soon become diamonds,
continents are omelettes,
the seas are just a squish of blue.

Space is layered with velvet,
the stars greet me,
the harvest moon smiles from ear to ear.

I land on Planet Nothing,
where there are no craters,
no creatures, no sparkling rocks,
and certainly no toy shops.

I cannot see a froth of cloud,
I cannot hear a phrase of music,
I cannot smell popcorn.

My journey home is double quick,
the carpet feels cosy beneath my icy feet.

Cherub Bob Was a Slob

Cherub Bob was a slob,
he wiped his nose
on his sleeve.
He left his feathers out
in all kinds of weathers,
till they got a horrid disease.

Now Bob is more careful,
he uses cloud tissue
and spreads his wings
under trees, to dry in the sun
and when he has done,
he jumps off his golden trapeze.

Little People

There are little people in my bed,
I hear them every night.

They march along my pillow,
and swing on my reading light.

They're always there in the morning
when my eyes blink up and down.

Half of them have a silly smile,
the other half, a frown.

If I smile at the frowning half
they start to wriggle and squiggle.

If I laugh a belly laugh,
they giggle, and giggle,
and giggle, and giggle
and giggle.

There are little people in my bed,
I hear them every night.

We all go to sleep together,
with our eyes shut tight.

Holding Back Time

Last night we gained a jot of time,
Clocks were held to let
An extra second slip into our lives.

Time enough for feet to leave the ground,
For fingers to click,
For an unkind word to be said.

Time for a mouth to open,
For a bee to land on a zinnia,
For a door to slam after a row.

Time for an eye to blink,
For a finger to push a piano's Middle C,
For the penny to drop.

Time for an apple to drop from the tree,
For a swing to swing,
For someone to change their mind
About saying that unkind word.

We have a leap second to make use of,
A jumping off point into our world.
What will you do with it?

Every few years we gain a second – called a leap second – to keep up with the varying rotation of the earth. This poem was written Sunday 1st July 2012.

Timing Is Everything

There's a time to tell your friend he's doing good,
And a time to tell your friend he's doing wrong.
There's time to eat broccoli,
And a time to eat milk chocolate.
There's a time to laugh out loud,
And a time to cry inside.
There's a time to wear a sparkly dress,
And a time to wear torn jeans.
There's a time to keep your favourite toy,
And a time to give it away.
There's a time to dance and jump and sing,
And a time to sit quietly and think.
There's a time to be angry and row,
And a time to make up and hug.
There's a time to sow a seed and watch it grow,
And a time to harvest its fruits.

Storing Time

(In answer to the question 'What happens to time after it is spent?')

All last year's nights
are in black bags
at Euston.

Paddington houses Lost Time
in rows of sieves
beyond Lost Property.

Bright sparkling mornings
are in clear plastic pockets
lining each horizon.

Birthdays are the grains
of gunpowder cracking fire
from Roman candles.

Moments of supreme happiness
are held in bubbles
rising from the mouths of guppies.

Sadness lives in cinders
waiting to be steamrollered
beneath the road.

Each and every
touch and hug and kiss and smile and sneeze,
is dancing with the dragonflies, up and down the breeze.

For Christmas

I give you a wooden gate
to open onto the world,

I give you a bendy ruler
to measure the snow that swirls,

I give you a prestidigitator
to make your woes disappear,

I give you a hopping robin –
he'll be your friend throughout the year,

I give you a box of mist
to throw over past mist-akes,

I give you a slice of ice
to slide on mysterious lakes.

Putting Away Christmas

The cards sit in a pile – a child,
dressed as a Christmas pudding,
walks along the top.

The tree lies outside –
pointing the way
for a council collection.

The fairy lights are curled up
inside their plastic box,
resting their filaments for another year.

Time to fold gold wrapping into bags,
read instructions on presents,
press my finger

on the last crumbs
of the Christmas cake,
and lick the sweetness away.

The 'I'm Not Tired' Dance

For Moniza

I've been to the park to-day,
swung on the swings,
slid down the slide,
climbed a tower,
I'm not tired.

I've been to school to-day,
run in the playground,
listened to teacher,
written a poem,
I'm not tired.

I got home to-day,
watched some telly,
drew a picture,
read my book,
I'm not tired.

I've eaten my dinner,
thrown my clothes,
had my bath,
cleaned my teeth,
coloured my nails,
talked to the gerbils,
danced on my bed,
blown my nose
and I'M NOT TIRED.

Tin Lid

Underneath the bedclothes late at night
I read by the light of a torch –

no giveaway crack that way
of light from my bedroom door.

If the battery was flat I'd chance my arm
with an old tin lid from a jam pot.

Stealing birthday candles
from the kitchen drawer

I'd melt each end on the lid.
Under the covers, the candles lit,

I read my books at this altar.
The thing set alight was my mind.

Lullaby

Forget about your homework,
forget about that fight,
give it up to the cheesy moon
and the meteor showers of night.

Chuck your frustrations out of the window,
punch your pillow with your fright,
then lie in a river of watercress,
tomorrow will be alright.

What Does Poetry Do?

It nosedives from the top of the fridge
into a bowl of rapids,

it crawls along the floor
and taps you on the knee,

it changes the colour of a room,

it puts great wheezing slices of life
into bun trays, with or without punctuation.

It manages this all by itself.

Acknowledgements

Many of these poems were published in the collections *Now You See Me, Now You ...* (Rabbit Hole Publications, 2002), *I Don't Want an Avocado for an Uncle* (Rabbit Hole Publications, 2006) and *The Humpback's Wail* (Rabbit Hole Publications, 2010).

'Sky High' was animated for the BBC CBeebies TV programmes *Poetry Pie* (2009) and *Rhyme Rocket* (2012)

'Files Not Found on a Computer' and 'My Cousin' were published in Issue 3 of *The Scrumbler*, 2010

'Gales of Laughter' was published in the Wenlock Poetry Festival Anthology 2012, and performed by The Archers actress Carole Boyd at the festival anthology launch event.

'Files Not Found on a Computer' was also published in *A First Poetry Book* (Macmillan, 2012) edited by Gaby Morgan and Pie Corbett.

'The Solar Powered Fairy' and 'I Can't Fix Everything' are featured poems on The Scrumbler 2013 website (*www.thescrumbler.com*).

'Rain in Nice' was published in *Lyrical Beats* (Rhythm & Muse, 2012) edited by Alison Hill

Biography

Chrissie Gittins was born in Lancashire and lives in Forest Hill, South London. Her children's poems have been widely anthologized, broadcast on BBC Radio 4 and animated for CBeebies. Chrissie won the Belmont Poetry Prize for children's poems in 2002. Her first children's collection *Now You See Me, Now You ...* (Rabbit Hole, 2002) was shortlisted for the inaugural CLPE Poetry Award in 2003; republished in 2009, it was selected as a Poetry Book Society Choice for the Children's Poetry Bookshelf. Her second children's poetry collection *I Don't Want an Avocado for an Uncle* (Rabbit Hole, 2006) was shortlisted for the CLPE Poetry Award 2007 and was a PBS Choice for the Children's Poetry Bookshelf. Her third children's collection *The Humpback's Wail* appeared in 2010 and was also a PBS Choice for the Children's Poetry Bookshelf. In 2012 Chrissie made an hour's recording of her children's poetry for the Poetry Archive.

www.chrissiegittins.co.uk

on Twitter: *@Armandii*

What people say about Chrissie...

'Magic, pure and simple.'
Sue Arnold, The Guardian

'For gentle but often surreal language, little people should sit cross-legged on the carpet with a copy of Chrissie Gittins's latest poetry collection. As a poet who regularly visits schools, award-winning Gittins knows how to help children let their imaginations wander'.
Helen Brown, Telegraph

'Chrissie Gittins knows just what words can do: she makes them dance, sing, sit still for a moment and then leap across the page with joy!'
Ian McMillan

'... a lot of ripe good ones'
John Hegley

'Poet Chrissie Gittins has a brilliant sense of humour and her quirkiness gallops across every page of this most original collection which is stuffed with daft moments and some serious ones too.'
Fiona Waters, CLPE Poetry Award